Notebook
for introverts

- This NOTEBOOK belongs to -

____